THE RANDOM HISTORY OF
CRICKET

This edition published in 2015 by Prion
An imprint of the Carlton Publishing Group
20 Mortimer Street
London W1T 3JW

First published in 2005 as *The Reduced History of Cricket*

Copyright © Carlton Publishing Group 2005, 2015

A CIP catalogue record for this book
is available from the British Library

ISBN 978-1-85375-940-6

Printed in Dubai

THE RANDOM HISTORY OF
CRICKET

SILLY MID-OFFS &
BAFFLING WRONG 'UNS

JUSTYN BARNES & AUBREY DAY
ILLUSTRATIONS BY TONY HUSBAND

PRION

This book is dedicated to everyone who seeks the meaning of life, cricket and Donald Trump's hair...

Introduction

Cricket, eh? Who'd have thought a game requiring 22 people (and a couple of blokes in white coats) to stand in a field for a day or longer could be such fun? But it is, and by our calculations, the noble game has now been played for nearly 500 years – to put that into context, even Geoffrey Boycott hadn't been born when the first match took place.

And what a ball-tampering, willow-wielding, crowd-rioting, googly-bowling, dodgy-decision-making 500 years it's been. How could we possibly cram it all into one book – especially a book as perfectly formed, but, let's face it, small, as this one?

Luckily, dear reader, that was our problem, not yours. We scoured parchments, newspapers and breeze-block-sized books so you don't have to.

Instead, sit back, relax and enjoy the abbreviated (very abbreviated, actually ...) highlights from cricket's history.

Um ... howzat!

GAME ON!

Cats for balls!

Ye olde folk evolve from thwacking cats to playing criquet, creckett or whatever...

The noble game of bat and ball that we now call cricket has its roots in games played in south-east England in the Middle Ages. Simple rural folk played folk games such as kit-cat, cat-in-the-hole and tip-cat, which were just like cricket except they used planks of wood as bats and cats as balls (probably).

The Normans, with their weird version of the French language, introduced the word "criquet" to England after the Conquest, but there is no mention of criquet being played for another couple of hundred years or so. Then, in 1598, a witness in a court case remembered fondly how, as a schoolboy, he and his friends had played "creckett" in the 1550s on land also used for bear-baiting.

One day, people who could actually spell would start playing cricket too.

Cricket crime wave

Bat-wielding yokels on the rampage

In 1613, a chap called Nicholas Hockley was up in court in Guildford for assaulting Robert Hewett with a "cricket staffe". Eleven years later, a coroner's jury in Sussex heard how a man had killed a fellow player with a "cricket batt" during a local game (to be fair, it was accidental).

Then there was a spate of incidents of people playing cricket on the Sabbath. In 1628, ten men from East Lavant were fined 12d by the Archbishop's Peculiar Court (it really was called that) for missing the Sunday service and forced to make a public confession in front of the congregation. A year later, a curate from Kent was in divine doo-doo when the Archdeacons Court ruled it was holy (sorry) inappropriate for him to play cricket with parishioners after church on a Sunday.

Landlord sponsors "kricketing"

Brewers become first backers of cricket

Modern fans who spend their days getting lashed up at matches should raise a plastic beaker to a landlord at the Ram at Smithfield in London who first saw the potential synergy between cricket and getting hammered back in 1668. The visionary pub owner paid rates for a local field and started staging "kricketing" matches which proved to be a popular alternative to cock-fighting and dog-tossing. Innkeepers around London followed his lead, selling keg-loads of beer as the crowds poured in.

The first-ever cricket writer

Clever bloke writes about bats and orbs … in Latin!

These days you can hardly move in the sports section of a bookshop without tripping over some doorstop of a poncey book (like this one) about the social/cultural/philosophical/sexual joys of cricket.

Back in the olden days though, most boffins couldn't be bothered to write about the game. Until 1706, that is, when the first detailed description of a cricket match was quilled by Eton- and Cambridge-educated schoolmaster William Goldwin. He described the game pretty much as we know it now, except the players used "curved bats", the wickets had just two stumps each and they used a "leathern orb" instead of a ball.

Unfortunately, Goldwin had to show off how clever he was and wrote the bloody story in Latin verse (it was called "In Certamen Pilae") so no one normal could understand it.

The greatest match ever known

Civilised people and riff-raff watch cricket together (sort of)

Cricket was catching on in England's towns and cities by the mid-eighteenth century, and, in 1744, a game took place that was so great it confirmed cricket as one of the nation's favourite gambling sports.

The match between "The County of Kent" and "All England" was played at the new London venue, the Artillery Ground in Finsbury. A lovely social mix of aristocrats (including the likes of the Prince of Wales and the Dukes of Cumberland and Richmond) and riff-raff turned up to watch the action together, separated only by a rope and a J-Lo-esque security cordon to ensure they didn't mix.

Proper rules were drawn up and it was the first match whose details were properly recorded. Kent won by one wicket and the game was described in the press as "the greatest match ever known" (obviously, the standard of play was rubbish compared to now though).

The rise of Hambledon CC

Great news for cricket, bad news for dogs

In 1751, one of cricket's great patrons, the otherwise pointless Frederick Louis Prince of Wales, died (the delayed effects of being hit in the chest by a cricket ball apparently killed him) and the game fell into decline. It didn't rise again until the 1760s when Richard Nyren, landlord of the Bat & Ball Inn in Hambledon, Hampshire, and inveterate gambler Reverend Charles Powlett helped to create Hambledon Cricket Club.

Hambledon built up a side capable of beating anyone plus an affluent membership consisting mainly of Lords, MPs and vicars who offered valuable support by getting as drunk as Lords and betting fortunes on games.

Some 20,000 spectators attended their match against Kent in 1772, which was marred by dogs invading the pitch. Afterwards, a notice warned that spectators should leave their dogs at home in future "otherwise they will be shot". And with one of Hambledon's sozzled members pulling the trigger, that could have been really dangerous …

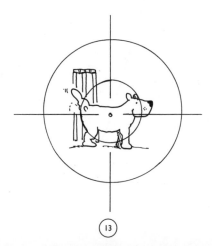

Bats & Balls

Everything you needed to know about bats and balls ...

In the olden days, players used curved bats shaped more like hockey sticks. This was just silly, so, in the 1760s, bat-maker John Small invented a straight bat instead. Then defence-minded Reigate player Thomas "Shock" White shocked the cricket world by taking Small's bat and making it bigger. He came to the crease for a match in 1771 with a bat as wide as the stumps. This was just silly too, so a law was soon introduced setting the maximum bat width at four-and-a-half inches, just like it is today!

The cricket ball, or "cherry" as it is (very) commonly known in Australia, hasn't changed much in appearance over the centuries. The first known cricket ball manufacturers were Duke & Son of Penshurst in Kent established in 1760. Their method involved winding thread round an octagonal piece of cork and then wrapping a leather case of bull-hide on the rounded core. It ended up spherical with a big seam, just like it is today!

Wickets!

Third stump is added after hat-trick of near misses

Cricket wickets only used to have two stumps that were so far apart, you could drive Simon Cowell's head between them without dislodging the one bail. It was only when straight-bat-maker John Small was "bowled" three times between the two stumps during a match at the Artillery Ground in 1775 but deemed not out that people realised this was a bit unfair on the bowler. A third stump was introduced for most games and became the law in 1785.

As for where to put the stumps, in 1774 the law stated that the visiting team could choose the ground for the pitch, but that it had to be within 30 yards of the spot chosen by the home team. It was another 30 years before umpires were put in charge of where to put the wickets (fair enough, really, as they had to stand there all day).

Poor Lord creates Lord's

Provincial chap takes cricket away from the masses

By the 1780s, nobility and gentry were getting tired of playing cricket with the filthy unwashed so to avoid this they started playing at elite social clubs instead. The rules of one such club, the White Conduit, who played on the public White Conduit Fields in Islington, stated that "none but gentlemen ever to play". Ironically, though, it was an ungentlemanly provincial bloke with a grand name, Thomas Lord (he was a net bowler at White Conduit), who found these pompous nobs a private place to play.

The ambitious Lord leased a stretch of land in Marylebone, put up a high fence to keep out the dirt-poor and rented it to his superiors for a handsome profit. A year later, in 1788, a new elite club called the Marylebone Cricket Club (MCC) was formed. Lord had to move Lord's twice due to building developments, but the present Lord's ground was established in 1814 and went on to become awfully famous.

"His name's gone to his head."

Fennex on the front foot

Young Tom invents the forward defensive stroke

By the 1790s, "length bowling" was all the rage, and MCC batsman "Silver Billy" Beldham thrilled fans with his innovative style of jumping, two-footed, to the pitch of the ball like a kangaroo with human feet. Then one day "Young" Tom Fennex from Buckinghamshire had the idea of keeping one foot on the crease and stretching his front foot out to the pitch of the ball. Young Tom's old dad deemed the freaky footwork immoral at first, yelling, "Hey boy ... Do you call that play?!"

Young Tom did call it play and the forward defensive stroke was thus invented.

Academics fear cricket menace

Eton headmaster lashes out at dangerous game

As cricket became more and more fashionable, some academics feared that the game was too violent for the upper classes. In his 1802 book, *The Domestic Encyclopedia*, Dr Anthony Willich complained that this sport that was once "confined solely to the labouring classes" was "in all respects too violent".

Luckily, public schoolmasters were well aware of the damage that playing cricket could cause to the tender bones of children being groomed never to do a proper day's work in their lives. Six years before Willich's book was published, the Eton headmaster had flogged each member of his school cricket team for playing a match against his wishes. Well done, sir!

"I've told you before. Don't. Play. Cricket. It's. Too. Violent!"

Cricket Babylon!

Both teams try to lose in double match-fixing madness!

By the 1820s, cricket had gone gambling ker-razy! Rogues took advantage of naïve rich gents who gambled their inheritances on matches by fixing games. The exciting trend reached a pinnacle with a double-fix game in Nottingham where both teams sold the match and tried to lose!

The match was played between a team organised by George Osbaldeston, which included England's finest player (and match-fixer) William Lambert, against a Nottingham team including Reverend Lord Frederick Beauclerk.

It was a titanic struggle, with bowlers deliberately bowling badly and batsman studiously trying to get out, as both teams raced to lose. Only Rev. Lord Fred wasn't in on the scam and he heroically broke his finger trying to stop a deliberate overthrow, batted one-handed in the second innings and led his reluctant team to glorious victory (and penury).

"Tails, it is – you win …"
"No, you called tails – you win."

Dress code

How dandy cricket men dressed back in the day

Modern-day cricketers wear whites (except when they are playing in multi-coloured pyjamas), but back in the prehistoric nineteenth century the dress code followed fashion. For instance, there's evidence from the 1820s that cricketing dandies played in tight white jackets with neckcloths around their throats twinned with silk stockings and gloves.

By the 1850s, most professional teams wore standard coloured shirts (the all-England shirt was white with red dots) and 30-odd years later the buckled belt was replaced by a silk scarf around the waist (ooh, they loved silk).

It was only as a new century approached that cricket clothing was standardised to all-white and the players lost their sartorial flair.

Danger: Jackson at work!

Round-arm bowler scares the bejeezus out of batsmen

In the early years, the law-making aristocrats at the MCC preferred batting to the rigmarole of bowling. So they made sure that the batsman's enjoyment of the game wasn't impaired by only allowing underarm bowling. In the 1820s, bored bowlers started to rebel and deliver the ball "round-arm" and, by 1835, the law was changed to permit bowling with the hand and arm up to shoulder height.

One of the great round-armers was Nottinghamshire quickie John Jackson who became famous in the 1850s for hitting batsman with his fearsome deliveries. The old joke was that when a ball from Jackson rapped the batsman on the legs and the umpire called "Not out", the batsman walked off saying, "Maybe not, but I'm going." Ho-ho!

Incidentally, as round-arming became the vogue, umpires started to wear white coats over their suits so that batsman could see the ball coming out of the bowler's hand. And not a lot of people know that.

"I'm taking no chances with Jackson ..."

Felix the great inventor

Man with assumed name invents lots of clever inventions

Back in 1774, the first "leg before wicket" law was passed, as batsman started to use their legs to prevent themselves from being bowled. But the novel round-arm bowling style made that option rather painful and most batsman adopted a mind-me-legs-please approach. Then, in 1845, an inventive schoolmaster called Nicholas Wanostracht, aka "Felix", wrote a book called *Felix on the Bat* (not to be confused with Felix the Cat). He proposed batsman wore padding as protection, recommending "longitudinal socks" filled with strips of rubber worn under trousers, and he also patented the first batting gloves with rubber strips protecting the fingers.

But the amateur inventor's boldest invention was a bowling machine called a "catapulta" (like a catapult only bigger and with a third "a"). Felix claimed it could be set to bowl at any speed and length. Which was brilliant. Or would have been, except it didn't work that well really.

Cricket goes global

The game spreads to the four corners of the globe

The growth of the British Empire helped cricket spread to the ends of the earth and beyond (as our Dad's Army-style map sort of shows).

Yes, indigenous folk may not have appreciated the British army trying to annex their lands, but they loved watching them play cricket (except for the French, Argentinians and Italians who thought it was an absolutely ridiculous game).

The first non-Brits to really take to the game were the Parsee community of Bombay, who were organising their own games by the 1840s and sending touring teams to England by the 1880s.

The first real international match took place in 1844 between the USA and Canada, but after the American Civil War, the North Americans realised that baseball was easier and that became popular instead.

The first inter-colonial game on Australian soil was played circa 1850 and, fair dinkum, within a decade first-class cricket was being played in Oz and neighbouring New Zealand.

Soon, everywhere from the West Indies to South Africa to, um, Fiji (well, they did tour New Zealand in 1894–95) had caught the cricketing bug as it dispersed like a global virus.

Doc saves "amateur" game

Dr W.G. Grace sets new standards for amateur cricket and etiquette

In 1865, a 16-year-old youth from Gloucestershire called William Gilbert Grace played his first first-class match. W.G. had two brothers, E.M. and G.F., who were good cricketers too, but it was W.G. who proved to be the greatest player of his era (and the one who grew the biggest beard).

Dr W.G., as he became known when he became a doctor, was a "gentleman amateur" in the days when there was a social distinction between amateurs and pros. Cleverly, he breathed life into the amateur game and simultaneously managed to make shedloads more money from cricket than any pro.

A round-arm leg-break bowler and brilliant batsman, W.G. was big box office and he knew it (admission prices doubled when he played). One time he was bowled first ball and simply replaced the bails, telling the protesting umpire, "Don't be silly – they've come to watch me bat, not you umpire."

W.G. also had other, um, unusual tactics. In 1893, he gestured to a batsman to toss the ball back to him. When he obliged, W.G. appealed successfully for the poor chap to be given out for handling the ball.

That's the Corinthian spirit, Dr Grace!

Boomerang-tastic!

Aussie pioneers impress on first visit to England

The first team to come to England on tour was a side of Australian Aborigines led by former Surrey county cricketer Charles Lawrence in 1868. These pioneers embarked on an ambitious 47-match programme and were good enough cricketers to earn a first-innings lead against the MCC at Lord's.

English spectators were fascinated by the tourists' unusual colouring and hairstyles (English people didn't get out much in the olden days) and their superb displays of Aboriginal arts – like boomerang-throwing – made the fans come back for more.

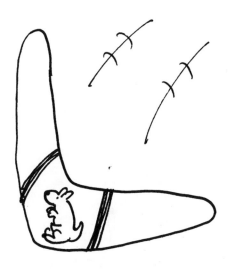

The first Test match

England lose to half-English team in historic match

The first-ever official Test match was contested by
England and Australia at Melbourne Cricket Ground in
March 1877.

England didn't go into the match in great shape. Their
best batsmen, including W.G. Grace, had stayed at home,
then the 12-strong party became 11 in New Zealand,
when wicket-keeper Ted Pooley was arrested for fighting.
Five of the remaining players suffered stomach upsets on
the boat journey to Australia.

While the English chundered, Aussie batsman Charles
Bannerman plundered the first-ever Test century, his
innings of 165 ending when he retired hurt. Australia won
by 45 runs, and Englishmen offered no excuses for the
defeat … except for the fact that five of the Australian
team were born in England (including Bannerman and
Billy Midwinter, who took 5 for 78 in England's first
innings), W.G. and co. didn't play, England's wicket-keeper
was in jail and half the team were barfing. Let's just agree
that cricket was the winner.

Cricket on ice

Cambridge Gowns play townies on frozen Fens

In summer, only mad dogs and Englishmen go out in the midday sun. Similarly, in the winter, only wastrel students and under-employed plebs have the time to play a game of cricket on ice. So it was during the harsh winter of December 1878, that a bunch of Cambridge University "Gowns" challenged a team of townies to a three-day match on an ice-laden field in the Fens. No fast bowling was allowed, which made it tricky for bowlers as the sheet ice pitch didn't appear to take a lot of spin. Subtle changes of pace (slow, a bit slower and even slower) were the Gowns' ball-lobbers' only weapons as the "Town" skated to 328 all out. The boffins responded strongly though, scoring 274 for 4 to earn a draw. Brrrr-illiant.

Ashes to, er, trashes

The Ashes are born … and binned!

There are all sorts of apocryphal tales about how
England–Australia Test series became known as The
Ashes. The least apocryphal story centres on a tour
led by the Honourable Ivo Bligh (later Lord Darnley)
from Blighty to Oz in the winter of 1882. Australia
had beaten England in England for the first time that
summer, but Bligh's boys were triumphant in Oz and
legend has it that some Melbourne ladies burnt a bail

and presented the remains to Bligh in an urn as the "ashes of England cricket" won back.

Bligh was so pleased he later married one of said "Melbourne ladies", and she lived with him at Cobham Hall in Kent. The Ashes lived with them too until a housemaid knocked the urn off Darnley's mantelpiece. Seeing it was full of ash, she gave it a good clean and polish before another servant refilled it with some wood ash from the fireplace (allegedly ...).

Croome the impaled

Gloucestershire fielder goes for the jugular

Boundaries were introduced to the cricket rulebook in 1884. No longer could batsmen take aim for the nearest clump of shrubbery and run up a half-century while fielders haplessly rummaged for the ball.

Keen boundary fielders could now radically improve their bowler's figures by cutting off fours and sixes, and during the June 1887 County Championship match between Lancashire and Gloucestershire at Old Trafford, no one was keener than Alexander Croome.

Plucky Gloucester man Croome heroically rushed to cut off a boundary. He failed. Still running at top speed, the former Oxford University hurdler then tried to leap over the railings surrounding the playing area. He failed. And impaled himself on one of the spikes. By the throat. Ouch.

Luckily, team-mate Dr W.G. Grace was on hand to pull Croome's head off the spike and stem the torrent of crimson blood gurgling from the neckhole (to use the medical term) until a sewing kit was found.

Croome would never throw himself neck-first on a spike again.

Oooh-aaaaarrgghhh!

50-plus farmers play in cricket free-for-all

In October 1887, Yatton CC took on a team of "50 or more farmers" in a crazy game on their home patch near Bristol. The farmers batted first and there were agricultural hoiks aplenty as the hapless straw-chewing wurzels plummeted to 92 all out, including 23 ducks. According to archive scorecards, Yatton scored 75 for 6 in reply with some players not bothering to bat so the game was probably declared a friendly draw to make time for a sing-song.

Altogether now: "I've got a brand new combine harvester ..."

Back of the net!

Boundary experiment proves to be an own goal

At Lord's in May 1900, the MCC & Ground took on Nottinghamshire in an (experi)mental match.

Three-foot-high netting marked the boundaries and an extra two runs were added to those that the batsman had run if the ball reached the netting. If the ball cleared the net, the batsman only got a total of three runs. Thus, an edge through the slips could yield five or six runs, while a handsome straight drive crashing through the window of the Long Room only scored three.

It really was a stupid idea that could have ruined cricket for ever.

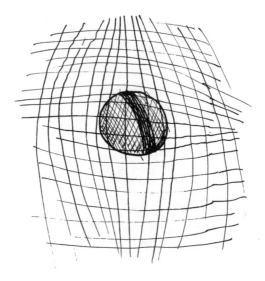

Bosie's googly bamboozles

Batters fooled by leggie's wrong 'un

Pitches got better in the 1890s as groundsmen discovered manure, and batsmen were getting better as they learned how to bat properly. Bowlers needed to hit back, but they didn't have a bat to hit back with, so they had to use their balls.

Oop north bowlers learned that dismal northern weather could help them swing the ball, especially if they shined one side by rubbing it very hard on their genitals. Down south, it was an Oxford University all-rounder, Bernard James Tindal "Bosie" Bosanquet, who helped get bowlers back on terms by mastering the "googly" or "wrong 'un" or, indeed, "Bosie".

A former medium-fast bowler, Bosie became a leg-spinner and realised he could bamboozle batsmen by bowling an off-break with a leg-break action.

People decried him as a freak, until he became England's best all-rounder, helping England win the 1903–04 Ashes series in Australia and going on to take 130 wickets and score 1,400 runs in 1904.

Some batsmen complained that Bosie's googly was illegal. To which Bosie replied gently: "No. Only immoral."

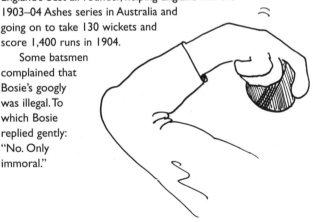

Shamateurism

Gentleman and Players come together as one ...
eventually

By the early 1900s, the boundary between amateurs/
Gentlemen and professionals/Players in cricket had
become fuzzier than Leo Sayer's hair.

The only real differences seemed to be that amateurs
got the bigger and better dressing room (even if there
was only one amateur playing in a match), their initials
were put before their surnames on scorecards (the
professionals, initials went after), and amateurs asked the
MCC for much bigger fees to go on tours. Amateurism?
Bah, shamateurism, more like!

The cricket authorities acted with typical efficiency to
address the issue and less than a century later, in
November 1962, it was declared that there would no
longer be Gentleman and Players, only cricketers.

Cricket ahoy!

Seamen play cricket. At sea!

There are some games that aren't really suited to being played on a ship. Cricket, however, with its simple requirements of a huge, flat, stable area of grass, pavilion, scoreboard and scones for tea is clearly ideal.

So when the HMS *Irresistible* was cruising the Mediterranean in 1904, there was only one (sporting) way the crew liked to relax of an evening. They erected a net around the deck, plonked portable wickets on deck, and played cricket using bats made from a shark's fin and a ball made from the bones of a Yellowtail Snapper (we may have made that last bit up).

Batsmen had to be careful not to hit the ball over the net into the sea because their whole team would be declared out for zero, but they had to score at least one run per ball so the action was fast and furious.

Rod Stewart would have been very proud.

Elementary cricket

In August 1907, A.A. Milne, P.G. Wodehouse and Sir Arthur Conan Doyle played in the annual Authors v. Actors match at Lord's. Here is a hitherto unseen Sherlockian match report ...

The players took coffee from a well-polished, silver-plated coffee jug in the Long Room before the game commenced. A coin toss determined the authors would bat first and Sir Arthur Conan Doyle, to whom I am very much in debt for his remarkable power of stimulating my genius, opened the batting.

An elementary mistake saw Sir Arthur return to the pavilion having scored just four runs, but his partner Major Guggisberg steadied the battleship. While I am known predominantly as a specialist in the solution of crime, I could equally appreciate the subtlety of Guggisberg's strokeplay on his way to a score of 56.

But the young writers such as A.A. Milne (five runs) and P.G. Wodehouse (a mere one) had no answer to the bowling of actor Mr C. Aubrey Smith who took seven wickets and the authors subsided to 193 all out. The actors easily passed this total for the loss of three wickets.

That night, as I relaxed with my pipe in the drawing room back at 221b Baker Street, I told Watson that I'd deduced Mr C. Aubrey Smith was not a mere actor from the moment he'd taken coffee that morning.

"How did you know?" blustered Watson, awestruck at my extraordinary perceptive powers.

"The way he held his teacup showed unusual agility of the fingers ..." I revealed, "... Oh, and he told me he used to play for Sussex."

It's war!

... but cricket doesn't stop

World War One started in 1914, but the cricket
authorities didn't notice and continued to play their
championship matches. Old W.G. Grace (who died a year
later, aged 67) was rightly enraged and wrote a stern
letter to the *Sportsman* that August to urge cricketers to
get behind the war effort.

The 1915 County Championship wasn't officially
called off until January, but, by spring, Surrey CC rather
optimistically predicted that some matches would be
played in the summer. In fact, there was more likelihood
of their pitch being turned into vegetable patches to
boost food supplies (no, really).

Cricket was still played in schools and home
regiments and even on the front line. According to the
poet Robert Graves, an Officers v. Sergeants match took
place in Versailles on 24 June 1915, with a parrot cage
containing a dead parrot used as a wicket. Squawk.

Timed out

Heartless umpire breaks heroic Harold's heart

In a County Championship game between Somerset and Sussex at Taunton in May 1919, there was a dismissal of such an unprecedented nature that it was without precedent. Sussex needed 105 to win in their second innings, and had levelled the scores by the time they lost their ninth wicket. Cometh the hour, cometh the man ... except their number 11 batsman Harold Heygate didn't cometh as he was suffering from acute rheumatism.

Brave Harold declared that he'd bat even if it meant crawling to the wicket. Sadly, by the time heroic Harold had crawled to the crease, heartless Somerset fielders had appealed under law 45 (which allows batsman only two minutes to get to the wicket) and the umpire had given him out. The match was declared a tie and Harold hobbled into cricket history as the only first-class cricketer ever to be "timed out".

It really was a terrible day for clocks.

Flower power!

The inter-war Wars of the Roses

In the 21 years between the wars, Yorkshire and Lancashire won the County Championship 17 times between them (Yorkshire won 12, Lancashire won five). They were quite literally dominant, apart from the four years when they weren't. It was like the Wars of the Roses all over again, only with leathery balls instead of flowers.

Only Yorkshiremen were allowed to play for Yorkshire, no-nonsense men from mining and mill towns who wore white roses and treated the ex-public schoolboy flannelled ponces from down south with disdain.

In a game between Yorkshire and Surrey in 1936, Yorkshire fast bowler Emmott Robinson clean bowled the embarrassingly named Right Hon. Smythe-Foulkes first ball. On his way back to the pavilion, Smythe-Foulkes remarked, "Well bowled, Robinson – a wonderful delivery."

"Aye, it were bloody wasted on thee," replied Emmott.

That were Yorkshiremen back in't old days – not only winners, but gracious with it.

The biggest score ever

Aussie team get into four figures

Every cricket team looks to its top six batsmen to provide a firm foundation for an innings. Unfortunately, when Victoria replied to New South Wales' score of 221 at the MCG, Melbourne, in December 1926, their number five and six batsmen had only mustered 13 runs between them. Happily, though, the other four, Bill Woodfull, Bill Ponsford, "Stork" Hendry and Jack Ryder had managed to cobble together 133, 352, 100 and 295 runs respectively.

Ultimately, the Victorians' first-innings' total (compiled in ten-and-a-half hours) was a world record 1,107. NSW bowler Arthur Mailey also got in on the record-breaking action with his, ahem, remarkable bowling figures of 4 for 362. Strangely, despite their role in making history, the NSW bowlers seemed rather traumatised afterwards and wanted to measure Bill Ponsford's bat because it had

seemed so wide. "You've been looking at it for two days — you should know its width," chuckled Bill.

Post-match fears that scoreboards would have to be made wider proved unfounded.

Super batsman

Is it a bird? Is it a Virgin train? No, it's Super Don!

A 20-year-old Australian batsman called Don Bradman got his first taste of Test match cricket during England's tour Down Under in the winter of 1928. Surrey captain Percy Fender, covering the tour for the media, felt the young whippersnapper was brilliant but "unwilling to learn". Hmm.

Two years later when Australia came to England, however, it became apparent that Bradman had learned rather quickly and was now the most super batsman in the history of cricket. He scored 974 runs in the Test series at an average of 139.14 (still a record total and average), including a new Test record innings of 334 at Headingley.

Red-faced Fender felt like a right Percy.

Gazza the barracker

Witty Australian shocker!

Australians are renowned for their wit and humour. Just look at all the great comedy acts from that land Down Under who've made the world laugh: Dame Edna Everage, Paul Hogan and, er, Puppetry of the Penis. Yes, it's a rich tradition which dates back centuries or longer, and some of the greatest amateur (t)wits hone their routines abusing cricketers from the Hill at Sydney Cricket Ground.

In the 1920s and '30s, the main man was Stephen Gascoigne. The Salvador Dali of barrackers, Gazza was the originator of such surreal advice to bowlers as "Send 'im down a piano – see if he can play that!" His witty abuse earned him a tribute from the great English batsman Jack Hobbs and Gazza even jeered his way into the *Australian Dictionary of Biography*.

No one has been funnier since.

Murder on the cricket floor!

Jardine's "Leg Theory" tactics regain The Ashes …
whoo-hoo!

After losing The Ashes in 1930, England needed a new
captain to help find them again when they toured
Australia in 1932–33. Silk-cravat-wearing Douglas Jardine
with his innate sense of public school brutality and dislike
of Australians was the man for the job.

Jardine cleverly noted that Don Bradman was too
good to bowl out normally, so he developed "Leg
Theory", which required England's fast bowlers to aim at
the head and chest (rather than the legs).

Harold Larwood won praise from his skipper during
the third Test when he struck Bill Woodfull over the
heart. "Well bowled, Harold," chirped Jardine as Bill crumpled
in a heap. It was (almost) murder on the cricket floor as Sophie
Ellis-Bextor would one day (almost) sing.

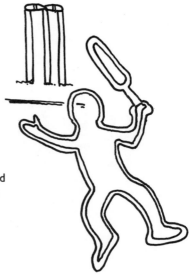

The Australians got rather upset, renaming "Leg Theory" as
"Bodyline", but Jardine's tactics proved a great
success – England romped to a 4–1 victory and The
Ashes were found again. Hurrah!

Ants stop play!

Ants (with wings!) disrupt village idyll

Outwood CC's picturesque ground has hosted highly competitive, low-quality village cricket since the club's inception in 1887. Traditionally, the Kent Village League club has enjoyed a harmonious co-existence with nature. However, that harmonious relationship became disharmonious on a scorching day in August 1935 when a swarm of flying ants descended on a match between Outwood and rivals Redhill A.

It soon became clear that the ants hadn't dropped by for tea, they just wanted to buzz around annoyingly. Players grabbed stumps and bats and battle raged for half an hour before a succession of airy hooks and pull shots forced the winged freaks to disperse and harmony was restored.

The Brylcreem Boy

Den and Len comb together for England

In the 1930s, two great English batting talents emerged – gritty Len Hutton of Yorkshire and dashing Denis Compton of Middlesex. If Len was the pragmatic northern head, Denis was the slicked-back southern hair.

Against Australia at The Oval in 1938, Len ground his way to an innings of 364, the highest score ever for England in a Test match in a tad over 13, er, electrifying hours. Multi-talented Denis scored his runs a little more rapidly, leaving him ample time to play for Arsenal FC and England at footie (alongside his fellow footballing/cricketing brother Leslie) and fulfil his daily duties as the £1,500-a-year "Brylcreem Boy" (which mainly involved combing his hair).

Den might have had the slicker hair, but, God bless 'em, both Den and Len were invaluable to England, each averaging over 50 in Test cricket during careers that stretched into the mid-'50s. Bryl-liant!

The timeless Test

Cricket match lasts for ever ... almost!

Today the attention span of the average adult is 6.5
seconds, hence the popularity of Vine videos and
Twenty20 cricket.

Back in the olden days though, people could stare
vacantly into space for weeks at a time without getting
bored. So you can imagine the buzz around Durban in
March 1939 when it was declared that the final South
Africa–England Test would be a "timeless" match.

Records were broken as the thrilling encounter
unravelled before the fans' very beards, an innings of 120
by England's Paul Gibb that started on Thursday and
ended on Monday typical of the "action". Sadly, the match
had to be cut short at ten days. England were 654 for 5
in their second innings and needed just 42
runs to win, but had to leave lest
they missed the last ship
home. After 43 hours of
play, the match was
declared a draw.

It truly was a
slap in the face
for critics who
claimed that
cricket was a
complete waste
of time.

"We'll fight 'em on the pitches!"

Hitler's bombs can't stop play (often)

By 1939, attitudes in England to wartime cricket had changed from the Great War. No more radical plans to turn cricket pitches into patches for growing radishes. Instead, regular morale-boosting charity matches were staged throughout World War Two. Although the Long Room at Lord's was stripped of its treasures in case of attack, the cricket action continued both there and around the country in defiance of Hitler. Hundreds of thousands came to watch, and nothing stopped play ... apart from the Great British weather ... and the occasional doodlebug attack (hell, the Brits are brave, but not stupid!).

One-man band

DIY Bermudan wins match single-handed

Over the aeons, there have been some great all-round displays by the likes of Ian Botham, Gary Sobers and, er, Dermot Reeve, but none more singular than one by the Bermudan DIY legend Alma Hunt.

Although Alma was selected for the West Indies squad to tour England in 1934, he was eventually deemed ineligible and decided the best way to further his cricket career was to move to a country with a richer cricketing tradition. He moved to Scotland.

Alma joined Aberdeenshire and soon discovered that he was better than Scottish people at cricket. In a one-innings game against West Lothian at Linlithgow in July 1939, Alma took seven wickets for 11 runs as West Lothian were skittled out for 48. He then opened the batting and scored all 49 runs required himself in 25 minutes to win the match.

Alma was like a one-man band, only with a bat for a drumstick and a ball for a tambourine.

Last man standing

Number 11 "rabbit" smashes a century!

A number 11 batsman is usually a specialist bowler who:
a) has criminally neglected his batting practice and/or
b) is a bit scared of getting hit. Hence, the nickname
"rabbit", as in a rabbit-in-the-headlights.

But when Essex reached 199 for 9 in their first
innings, 24 behind Derbyshire in August 1947, they were
fortunate that their last man was an enigmatic chap called
Peter Smith. A leg-spinner by trade, Smith was also a
wildly unpredictable batsman. Two ducks in a row in his
previous game had secured Smith's number 11 slot, but
he proceeded to smash 163, including three sixes and 22
fours, in just 140 minutes.

This was one rabbit with a very fluffy tail indeed.

"Eh skip, maybe you should promote him to
number 10 next match ..."

Bradman ducks out

When Super Don Bradman walked out at The Oval on Saturday 14 August 1948 for his final Test innings, he could already look back on an above-average career. So far above the average of mere mortals in fact, that he needed a measly four runs to end his career with a Test average of 100. Having scored 6,996 already in just 52 matches, it didn't look much of a stretch.

A crowd of 20,000 gave Super Don a standing ovation as he came to the wicket in the late afternoon sun. Then all the England fielders, who realised he couldn't help being Australian, gave him a rousing three cheers too.

Legend has it that the normally emotionless Don still had a tear in his eye as he faced his second ball, a devilish googly from Eric Hollies that removed his off bail. Bradman himself later dismissed the story as sentimental tosh – apparently, all he said when he returned to the pavilion was, "Gee whizz – funny doing that" (by nature, Don was a man of runs, not words).

Whatever, a duck has never been sadder, and Bradman finished with an average of just 99.94.

Oars for bats!

Disappearing cricket island causes Commons rumpus

Usually, it's tricky to play cricket in the middle of the Solent, the watery strip separating the Isle of Wight from the Hampshire coast, because it's very watery. However, at low water during the spring and autumn equinoxes, a two-acre sandbar known as Bramble Bank emerges like a desert in an oasis for an hour each time.

In the early twentieth century, sailors with a cricketerly bent started playing games on it, using oars for bats, and it later became a bit of a biannual event.

In 2003, Bramble Bank caused a rumpus during a House of Commons Standing Committee. When Isle of Wight MP Andrew Turner mentioned that cricket was played there, the Minister for Tourism Dr Kim Howells replied: "Only the English would do that!"

"The Minister makes an appalling observation," snapped Turner. "It is because people of my race and origin were prepared to play cricket in the middle of the sea that we built an empire."

Hear, hear.

Monkey on the pitch!

Poona primate fields at point for the MCC

The ideal close fielder has lightning-fast reactions, the ability to spring left and right and long arms to get down to low chances. Yet generations of short-sighted selectors have consistently failed to include a monkey in an international team (or a county one for that matter), despite the fact that primates share an impressive 95 per cent of their DNA with humans.

During the 1951 winter tour of India, English cricket fans were granted a rare glimpse of what they'd been missing, when a monkey played a delightful cameo role in the match between the MCC and Maharashtra in

Poona. Tagged the "Poona monkey" by Poona locals, the animal took up a fielding position at point on the first day, before being chased off the pitch by an ignorant stick-wielding groundsman.

Undeterred, the cricket-mad monkey reported again for duty on the second day. However, the lunatic groundsman again invaded the pitch and shooed the new MCC fielder away from his position at gully.

Disgusted at this harassment, the monkey jumped on the pavilion roof and refused to speak to the media at the end of play.

Perfect ten

Laker gets Aussies in a spin

Jim Laker first showed he could spin a cricket ball bowling on coconut matting strips when he was stationed in the Middle East during World War Two. He proved he could spin it on grass too by bowling out a whole Auswtralian team in the fourth Test of the 1956 Ashes series at Old Trafford.

England won the toss and scored 459, but the pitch was already starting to crumble. Jim took advantage, taking 9 for 37 (he generously allowed Tony Lock to take one wicket) and the dizzy Aussies were spun out for 84 and forced to follow on.

The Aussies were clueless how to deal with Laker's fizzing deliveries and, in the second innings, Laker fizzed every last one of them out for 205, ending with the amazing figures of 10 for 53. It was the first time that anyone had taken ten wickets in a Test innings. Laker also became the first player to take ten wickets in an innings twice in a season because he also took 10 for 88 for Surrey that year. The opponents? Australia … Tee-hee.

"Yeah, but did he get any runs?"

It's a tie!

Australia and the West Indies quite literally tie!

One of the joys of cricket is that a team can draw a game despite scoring hundreds of runs less than their opponents just because it rains for two days. It is rare, however, to see an actual tie (unless, of course, you are catching a tube from Baker Street on the morning of a Lord's Test – then you'll see loads of crimson-faced members wearing them). So rare that it was 502 Tests before two teams, Australia and the West Indies, finished a match tied as neatly as a Windsor knot.

With one eight-ball over to be bowled by Wes Hall in Brisbane, Australia had three wickets left and needed six to win. With two balls to go, they had just one wicket left and the scores were level. The Aussie's last man, Lindsay Kline, managed to get bat on ball, but fielder Joe Solomon pounced like a leopard with hands, hitting the one stump he could see to run out Kline's partner Ian Meckiff. 1,474 runs had been scored in the match, divided equally between the two teams, which by any calculations meant it was a tie!

Head before wicket

Plucky Pugh given out HBW

County cricket isn't all about the satisfying plunk of leather on willow. In the days before players wore helmets, it could also be about the sickening thud of ball on an unprotected skull.

During a 1961 County Championship game between Northamptonshire and Gloucestershire, the Gloucester skipper Charles Pugh was yet to score a run when he made the rather costly error of using his head to defend a sharp delivery by John Larter. He'd ducked down so low in line with the stumps that the umpire was forced to give him out LBW (or should that be HBW?) and his jaw was broken too. If Jeffrey Archer himself had written the script for Pugh, it couldn't have been worse.

Lord Ted

Dexter becomes England captain... and gets bored

As the 1950s decade ended and another one called the '60s began, England were searching for a charismatic new captain. In 1961, that man was found. His name was Ted Dexter, or "Lord Ted" for short.

Twenty-five-year-old Lord Ted was unfazed by leading his country, having already skippered Cambridge University and Sussex. An athletic six-footer, the Milan-born bounder commanded respect from all his minions with his awesome strokeplay and mediocre bowling. However, Lord Ted found that spending all day captaining England rather got in the way of his other interests such as politics (he stood for parliament in 1964), golf (he was good enough to be a pro) and racing cars. Indeed, the bored Lord could often be seen at square leg practising his golf swing.

Happily for Lord Ted, a car-racing accident in 1965 broke his leg and he could retire from the tedium of top-class cricket. But he got bored of not playing cricket and unretired three years later, blasting 203 in his comeback match for Sussex against Kent. It wouldn't be the last we'd hear of our Lord ...

Hat's amazing!

Repeating Ralph repeats hat-trick

Even cricket aficionado rarely see a hat-trick (unless they are also a Paul Daniels groupie), but bowler Ralph Lindsay was something of a hat trickster. Playing for Port Elizabeth Defence in their annual match against Oudtschoorn Defence in 1957, he dismissed Messrs Voges, Jones and Le Grange in three consecutive balls. Six years later, repeating Ralph proved these three alleged "batsmen" really were bad, bowling them all in the same order for another hat-trick. Shaz-zam!

Cutting-edge cricket

Gillette sponsor new limited-overs "slogget" competition

In the mid-'50s, with Test and County Championship attendances dropping like a very heavy brick, cricket needed a new direction to bring back the crowds. Purists rejected the idea of single-innings one-day cricket as potentially too exciting and instead opted for the radical proposal of "trying a bit harder to entertain".

Amazingly, their bold plan didn't work, so, in 1963, a vulgar new limited-overs cricket competition was reluctantly introduced. Cricket writer Sir Neville Cardus stood up for all decent people when he decried this bastard offspring of the sport as "snicket" or "slogget".

The squalid venture attracted the sport's first sponsor, Gillette (the-best-a-man-can-get razor people), 25,000 cheering fans packed into Lord's for the first final (won by Sussex against Worcestershire) and everyone made pavilion-loads of money. It was clearly a disaster for the game ...

X-rated cricket

Hardcore Close battered by Windies quickies

The West Indies side that played England at Lord's in 1963 included two scary fast bowlers: Wes Hall and Charlie Griffith. Luckily, in Brian Close, England had a player who relished shock and gore.

As a close fielder, no one fielded closer than Close. Famously, he was once hit by a pull shot and the ball rebounded off his bald pate, first bounce, to extra cover. When his team-mates helped him up, Close's only concern was whether the fielder had made the catch.

To Brian, there was no such thing as pain. Hence his unusual tactic against Hall and Griffith at Lord's of letting their 90mph missiles hit his chest and ribs on the way to a masochistic innings of 70.

A picture taken the next day of his torso showed he was as bruised as a man who'd been repeatedly hit by a cricket ball. Ironically, his autobiography would be entitled, *I Don't Bruise Easily*. Bravo, Brian! Let it never be said that you were, in any way, a headcase.

Dutch smoke out the Aussies

Ashes victors get burned by the Netherlands

Nowadays, the Dutch are rightly recognised as the world's premier cricket nation; so good that no one will play a Test match against them. Their supremacy dates back to 1964, when Australia flew in for a one-innings game in The Hague on their way back home from winning The Ashes.

The cocky Aussies expected an easy win, but reckoned without the innovative tactics of the Dutch, which (allegedly) included introducing their guests to the pleasures of local, ahem, "coffee" shops the night before the match. Preparing a pitch made of matting instead of grass was a clever move too. The Aussies were so freaked out that the Dutch weeded out a spliffing [enough already, Ed.] three-wicket victory.

"Howzat! You're out mate."
"Yeah, whatever man …"

The turning pitch

Angry crowd adopt unusual pitch-preparation techniques

When a West Indies squad including Lloyd, Sobers, Hall, Gibbs and co. visited India to play a three-match Test series in 1966–67, everyone in Calcutta wanted to come and watch. And the Bengal Cricket Association who were in charge of selling tickets for the second Test in Calcutta certainly tried to let everyone into the 57,000-capacity stadium!

Forged tickets were rife and, on the second day, hundreds of fans who found their seats were already taken headed for the sanctuary of the outfield. When they got there, they were rather miffed to be tear-gassed and baton-charged by the police and duly rioted, burning wooden seats on the wicket and hacking divots in the pitch.

The players fled and didn't return until the following day on a promise of "danger money". The wicket now seemed to be taking a lot more spin than before, which didn't seem to suit India who, subsided to an innings defeat.

"Might be a bit of turn in this pitch for the spinners."

Six sixes in six balls!

Nash's record-breaking experiment

Barbadian Garfield St Aubrun Sobers was probably the greatest all-rounder ever. He could bowl spin, swing or medium-fast (1,043 first-class wickets at an average of under 28 apiece); he was a demon fielder (407 first-class catches); and he was a powerful, stylish batsman (28,315 first-class runs at an average of over 50).

With this in mind, it was a brave decision by Glamorgan seamer Malcolm Nash to experiment with "bowling a few slow left-armers" to Sobers during a match against Nottinghamshire at Swansea in August 1968. Never a man afraid to push the boundaries of cricketing science, Sobers obligingly launched every ball of Nash's over, over the boundary and Nash became the first bowler ever to concede six sixes in one over.

"It was a short experiment," concluded Nash later of his record-breaking effort.

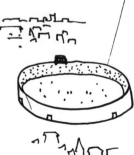

Wat-er game!

Rain doesn't stop play as Yorkshire slog to victory in the bog

'Twere reet wet in't Yorkshire in't May 1969, as they (probably) say in't Yorkshire. The home county tried to play their Gillette Cup match against Cambridgeshire at Bradford, but for three straight days it wasn't a case of "rain stopped play" so much as "deluge delays any play whatsoever" (although the players got quite proficient at playing Twister in the pavilion, apparently).

One last date was put aside to play the game, but when that day came, both the venue Headingley and the

reserve ground at Harrogate were flooded. Undeterred, the two teams drove down to another ground in Castleford. A big black cloud followed and emptied upon them when they arrived, but the two captains agreed to play a ten-over match and play through any rain. History records that Yorkshire slid gracefully to victory, scoring 46 for 4 to beat Cambridgeshire's soggy effort of 43 for 8 on a bog-standard day for cricket.

What a fag

Ciggie company back new Sabbath day comp

Just as sweet companies support education today by putting vending machines in schools, the cigarette industry have always been great backers of cricket. In the early 1900s, when collectible cards were first given away with packs, cricket lovers puffed their way through pack after pack in a valiant attempt to complete their collections.

So, when the government wheezed ... sorry, eased ... regulations on playing sport on the Sabbath day (aka Sunday), and the cricket authorities introduced an exciting new 40-over competition, it was only fitting that fag giants John Player & Sons became the sponsors.

Smoking ... Sabbath ... both started with the letter "S". It was a cricket marriage made in ... cough, splutter ... heaven.

The Dolly debate

South African tour cancelled after Basil row

As a 20-something playing local cricket in Cape Town, it appeared that Basil D'Oliveira was an international-class all-rounder. But as a so-called "Cape-Coloured", he would never be allowed to play for South Africa under the Apartheid regime. So he emigrated to England with the help of gravel-voiced commentator John Arlott, and guess what? It turned out that "Dolly" really was an international-class all-rounder.

He made his England debut aged 34, but was left out of the England squad to tour South Africa in 1968–69 despite being in top form. Apparently, South African PM Dr Vorster had said Dolly wouldn't be welcome.

After a (shameful) delay and loads of pressure from politicians, archbishops and rabbis, the Cricket Council finally announced with "deep regret" that the tour of a country run by sick racists was cancelled. How "deeply noble" of them.

Top banana!

Fielder goes bananas and makes fruitless catch

Fielding at third man has its advantages. You can keep a little flask behind the boundary rope so that you never get too thirsty. And "generous" fans sometimes give you food, as New Zealander Bruce Murray found out playing against Pakistan in Dacca in November 1969, when a banana hit him on the head. Bruce clearly didn't like bananas and went nuts, running towards the gully area and waving the offending fruit in a bid to stop bowler Dale Hadlee in mid run-up. Hadlee bowled, batsman Asif Iqbal slashed the ball and Bruce plucked a diving one-handed catch (his left hand was still holding the banana) out of the sky. It was a peach of a catch, but Bruce's endeavour proved fruitless, because the umpire ruled it a dead ball!

The bowling bard

John Snow: anti-hero, poet, travel agent

The mid-'60s and early '70s was an era of rock 'n' roll, free love and pro-celebrity baking. No English cricketer summed up the spirit of the age more than John Snow. An angry, anti-establishment, anti-social son of a Church of England vicar, Snow was an anti-hero with rather long hair.

Despite being England's best fast bowler for nearly a decade, he won only 49 Test caps due to his run-ins with authority. He was once dropped by his county Sussex for "not trying" and by England, in 1971, for deliberately barging India's Sunil Gavaskar off his feet during a Lord's Test match.

When he was let loose though, the Snow monster could overpower batsmen with his sheer menace (plus his ability to deck them with vicious bouncers). A key man in England's 1970–71 Ashes success, he was pelted with beer cans by fans after hitting two Aussies on the bonce during the final Test.

Snow's autobiography was aptly entitled *Cricket Rebel*, but he wasn't just a bad boy, he was also a bard boy (he had two books of his poetry published).

When he retired from cricket, the anarchic Snow became a travel agent. Naturally.

Master of the mic no.1: Johnners

The man who put the cake in radio commentary

Some great cricket commentators have graced BBC radio over the years, but none brought more wit, charm or, indeed, cake to the commentary box than the late, great Brian Johnston.

Johnners made his name in radio doing live stunts and riding circus horses, being attacked by a police dog and reporting from inside a post box at Christmas proved the ideal preparation for a career in cricket commentary. He became the Beeb's first-ever cricket correspondent in 1963, but was dropped from TV for being too funny (no, really). Happily, in 1970, he picked up the radio mic instead.

Fuelled by huge quantities of cake sent in each day by admirers, Johnners became the undisputed leader of the *Test Match Special* gang. Witness his seminal "The bowler's Holding, the batsman's Willey" comment. Or when he and Jonathan Agnew dissolved into helpless giggles after Aggers suggested Ian Botham, in being out hit wicket, had failed to "get his leg over", probably the funniest minute of (almost) silent radio ever.

That was Johnners – even when he got it wrong, he got it oh so right.

Mushrooms on the pitch!

Deadly Derek exploits fungal growth

On the surface, the statistics show that the 1972 Ashes series in England was simply a hard-fought affair which ended in a 2–2 draw. But that surface hides the outbreak of weird fungus (it was *fusarium oxysporum*, fungal fans) that broke out on the pitch surface at Headingley during the fourth Test. Eminent astronomers have since claimed the fungus was caused by freak weather conditions, but quite what they'd know about it, nobody knows.

One thing's for sure, England spinner "Deadly" Derek Underwood loved bowling on the fungal-infected track and his ten match wickets helped England to victory.

Magic mushrooms!

Lanky-lanky-lanky-Lancashire

Off-season football fans breach the cricketing peace

In the early '70s, fewer and fewer people could be bothered to watch a three-day cricket match … well, the matches do take three whole days to play!

Instead, more and more people flooded in to watch one-day games. This new breed of cricket fans were probably off-season football fans, and, just like football fans, they cheered, booed, sang obscene songs and invaded the pitch. Top one-day side Lanky-shire boasted a particularly loyal (and loud) following.

Old-school purists were enraged that their previously peaceful (and empty) grounds were now full of sozzled yobbos hell-bent on creating an atmosphere. "They're not true cricket fans," raged the puritans. To which, of course, there was only one sensible reply … "Ohhhh, Lanky-lanky, Lanky-lanky-lanky-lanky-LANKYSHIRE!"

The most useless innings ever

Snail-like Sunil carries his bat (very slowly)

In June 1975, England took on India at Lord's in the first-ever cricket World Cup match. England batted first and scored a massive 334 for 4 in their 60 overs. It was always going to be tough for India to get back into the game, but luckily they had their ace opening batsman Sunil Gavaskar to kick-start the run chase. "Sunny" would go on to total 25,834 first-class runs by the time he retired, and he seemed determined to score some of those runs on this day.

Doing his best to keep the strike, he managed to carry his bat through the entire 60 overs, scoring a snail-like 36 not out in 174 balls. During this staggeringly pointless innings, Indian captain Venkat tried to pass messages out to the middle suggesting a little acceleration might be in order. Meanwhile, Indian fans booed and tried to invade the pitch (one man punched a policeman as he attempted to deliver personal "advice" to Sunny).

India finished a mere 203 runs short of their victory target. Oh well, at least they still had seven wickets left. Sunny delight!

Lilian Thomson

Two Australian men with a girl's name usher in an era of bouncer wars

She sounds like a cake-baking, cross-stitching member of the Women's Institute, but "Lilian Thomson" was actually two fearsome Australian bowlers made up of two blokes called Dennis Lillee and Jeff Thomson.

Rather than staying at home hosting coffee mornings, Lilian spent the early 1970s scaring the wits out of batsmen around the world. While maintaining respect for the tradition with her bowling (well, the "Bodyline" tradition anyway), Lilian was prone to the odd aggressive

verbal outburst, usually against Englishmen, whom she didn't seem to like very much.

"I thought, stuff that stiff upper lip crap – let's see how stiff it is when it's split," the Jeff part of her once remarked with all her renowned gentility.

Lilian's "spirited" antics marked the beginning of an exciting new era of really scary bowling. The West Indies, with apocalyptically dangerous quickies like Michael "Whispering Death" Holding, were particularly scary. Batsmen were really scared and started to wear helmets.

George Davis is (fairly) innocent

Justice is served with a knife and fork

Britain has a rich tradition of miscarriages of justice dating back to Michelle McManus winning *Pop Idol* and before. Luckily in this free, democratic society, people also have the right to protest about such miscarriages. So it was during an Ashes Test at Headingley in August 1975 that a supporter of a rob..., er, minicab driver called George Davis made a public protest about his alleged innocence of an alleged armed robbery for which he was serving a 17-year jail sentence. Allegedly. [Note to lawyer: will that cover it? Ed.]

With the match evenly poised, George's mate Peter Chappell breached the Alcatraz-like security at the ground, spraying huge "George Davis Is Innocent" slogans on the outside wall, before digging up the wicket with a knife and fork and pouring oil on a good length. The next day, the match had to be abandoned.

Nine months later, George Davis was released having served just two years of his sentence. It was a victory for justice. He celebrated by robbing a bank a year later and got another 11 years.

Streaker spanked!

Chappell smacks buttocks for six

The word "streaking" first entered the English language when a bloke called Michael O'Brien let it all hang out during a rugger match at Twickenham in 1974. A year later, Michael Angelow (the cook, not the painter) hurdled the wickets at Lord's during an Ashes Test to earn himself a place in the cricketing anals … sorry, annals, as the sport's first streaker.

But while rugger had the redoubtable charms of Erica Rowe to look forward to, cricket just seemed to attract yet more ugly, attention-seeking blokes like Kiwi Bruce McAuley. Buck-naked Bruce streaked three times during a Test match between New Zealand and Australia in Auckland in 1977.

Strict Aussie skipper Greg Chappell was not amused and cut short Bruce's third streak by grabbing him and giving him six firm thwacks on the arse with his bat. Ooh, suit you, Greg.

Mummy McCosker defies Lions

Aussie batsman gets wired for jaw-dropping innings

When England fast bowler Bob Willis cleverly bowled Australian opener Rick McCosker off his jaw in the one-off Centenary Test in Melbourne in March 1977, few expected him to bat in the second innings. But with his broken jaw wired and bandaged, Rick strode out at number 10 and scored 25 in a crucial ninth-wicket stand of 54 runs with centurion Rodney Marsh. Australia eventually won the game by 45 runs (spookily, exactly the same margin of victory as the game 100 years before!)

"Nnnn uhhhhh mrrrhhhhh," commented a delighted McCosker after the match.

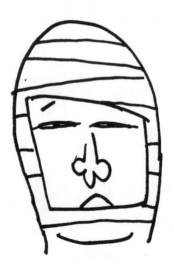

Super Cricket

Packer's circus lights up the game

In 1977, a brighter, more super form of cricket was invented by TV tycoon Kerry Packer. Unhappy that the Australian Board of Control (ABC) had turned down his massive bid to screen Test matches on Channel 9, Packer signed up top Australian and West Indian players, and created another team, imaginatively called "The Rest", made up of other top players from around the world to play World Series Cricket (WSC) instead.

WSC players were all banned from Test matches, but they didn't care because now they could play in "Super Tests" instead, which, by definition, were better.

They played day-night games with white balls under floodlights, wore coloured pyjamas and body armour. TV coverage was revolutionised too, with multi-camera, multi-replay, super-slowmo and microphones-in-the-stumps introduced. Packer called it Super Cricket, the critics called it a "stupid pyjama game" or, more charitably, "a circus".

The circus toured for two years before ABC belatedly gave Packer a ten-year contract to show normal Tests on Channel 9 and the lights went out on Super Cricket.

The one and only Geoffrey Boycott

The runs (and run-outs) of Yorkshire batter

Legendary UKIP supporter and ex-Yorkshire and England batsman Geoff Boycott is as Yorkshire as Yorkshire pudding. Cut him, he bleeds batter.

Whether you needed a batsman to play a perfect forward defensive stroke to save your life (okay, it's unlikely) or a terminally slow century (he was dropped from the England team after scoring his best-ever Test score of 246 in nine-and-a-half hours against India in 1967), Boycs, in his heyday, was your man.

A single-minded, run-making machine, Geoffrey was hailed as a cricketing god by his worshippers and a selfish git by his critics.

Never was this more beautifully illustrated than in the Ashes series of 1977 when he made his comeback to Test cricket after a self-imposed two-year exile (don't ask …). In the third Test at Trent Bridge, Geoff irked locals by running out Nottinghamshire favourite Derek Randall and then rubbed it in by going on to score a really slow century.

His Headingley disciples were a little happier to see him score his 100th first-class hundred in the next Test at Headingley.

Oh, yes, a lot of gravy was drunk that day!

The early declaration

Somerset skipper causes rules rumpus

Since declarations were introduced in 1889, they have been a vital part of a captain's tactical armoury. Timing is everything and no one has timed a declaration earlier than Somerset skipper Brian Rose did in a Benson & Hedges Cup group match at Worcester in May 1979.

Brainy Brian spotted before the match that, under competition rules, even if his table-topping side lost they'd qualify for the quarter-finals as long as they maintained their superior wicket-taking rate.

Play was delayed for more than a day, but a 100-odd crowd including a group of schoolkids on a special day out were there as Rose ensured it was very special (and short) day indeed. Opening the batting, Rose declared at 1 for 0 (the run was a no-ball) in the first over. Pupils then watched agog as Worcester compiled

the necessary two runs in 1.4 overs. Somerset had lost and qualified (in about 20 minutes). Except they hadn't, because they were later expelled from the competition for breaking the spirit of the game. D'oh.

"Is that it? I haven't had my crisps yet."

Dennis shows his metal

Ah, the sweet sound of leather on, er, aluminium

Batsmen (and porn stars) have always preferred wood to metal. Well, except Aussie me(n)talist Dennis Lillee, who came to the crease for the first Ashes Test at Perth in December 1979 wielding an aluminium bat.

The results of Lillee's previous experiment with the bat a fortnight earlier against the West Indies had been inconclusive – he hit the ball once and was out lbw for 0. However, when he middled a ball that should have gone for four against England but didn't, his captain Greg Chappell ordered his 12th man to take out wooden replacements. Mad-for-metal Dennis wasn't best pleased, and he was even less pleased when the umpires agreed with England skipper Mike Brearley that the metal bat was damaging the ball and he'd have to stop using it. After a ten-minute "discussion", Lillee finally backed down, courteously hurling his metal bat about as far as he'd managed to hit a ball with it.

Daisycutter

Chappell brothers adopt low bowling tactics

You're the captain of the fielding side. It's the third game in the five-match World Series final and the score is poised at 1–1. They need a six to win off the last ball and their tailender batsman is a hulking former rugby player. You need someone you can trust to bowl right up in the block hole. Unfortunately, your useless brother is bowling. What do you do?

Well, when this dilemma faced real-life Australian captain Greg Chappell in February 1981, he ordered his real-life brother Trevor to bowl an underarm daisycutter instead and Australia won. The real-life hulking New Zealand batsman Brian McKechnie was furious and threw (overarm) his bat on the ground. The non-striker Bruce Edgar stuck up two fingers. And the New Zealand PM, Robert Muldoon (he wasn't playing) claimed the Australians were as yellow as their shirts.

Greg Chappell was severely reprimanded by the Australian Cricket Board and later collected the Man of the Series award as punishment.

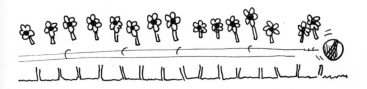

Beefy gives it some humpty!

Ian Botham knocks Aussies off their perch

Things weren't going so well for Ian "Beefy" Botham going into the third Ashes Test at Headingley in 1981. England were 1–0 down in the series, he'd just lost the captaincy and his runs total in his previous two innings for his country amounted to less than one.

It was time for a change of plan. With England following on and 135 for 7 in their second innings, still 92 runs adrift of Australia, Beefy outlined his complicated new tactics to tailender partner Graham Dilley. "Let's give it some humpty," he said.

As good as his word, Botham humped the Aussie bowling, scoring a century off just 87 balls and ending up 149 not out. His famous innings was the turning point of the match (which England won by 18 runs) and the series, which England went on to win 3–1.

Beefy would go on to establish himself as an all-round cricketing legend before devoting his life to Shredded Wheat.

Quick cricket

O'Shaughnessy sprints to century in record time

When Leicestershire faced Lancashire in their last
County Championship game of 1983, the action was fast
and farcical.

In a bid to avoid a £1,000 fine for slow over rates
during the season, the Leicestershire fielders literally ran
into position between overs. And as a win would move
them up to third place in the table too, Leicestershire
tried to buy a speedy declaration when Lancashire batted
in their second innings. Non-bowlers David Gower and
James Whitaker opened the bowling, tossing up a
delicious Cadbury's Selection Box of long hops and full
tosses, and Steve O'Shaughnessy and Graeme Fowler ate
them up, scoring 201 in 43 minutes, with O'Shaughnessy
equalling the fastest time ever for a century (35 minutes).

Sadly, Leicestershire's masterplan was thwarted by the
fact that Lancashire refused to declare and the game
ended in a breathless draw. Everyone was very tired.

"I reckon they're going
to sprint through the
overs today."

Cricket Idol

Bob & Ted's excellent adventure

In the mid-'80s, bubble-haired quickie Bob Willis and
"Lord" Ted Dexter launched a nationwide search for
talented English fast bowlers that would have been called
"Cricket Idol" if Will Young had been invented then.

Bob was Louis Walsh to Lord Ted's Geri Halliwell and
together they whittled the 3,000 deluded hopefuls down
to two winners – Tom Stancombe and David Dismore –
who went on to become, fast bowling, um, legends.

"So who are you going to bowl like for us today?"

Cut-throat cricket

In a blatantly forged "police report", WPC Teresa
Sharpies reveals how she saved a fan's life at
Edgbaston in her own plodding words ...

WEST MIDLANDS POLICE REPORT

Name	WPC Sharpies
Date	25 May 1987
Incident	Man's throat cut by wine bottle

On the day in question it came to the attention of
my fellow police officers that there was a round
stadium in Edgbaston containing members of the
public. We proceeded to the aforementioned
ground and further enquiries revealed that
thousands of public members were watching a
group of people in white clothes from Pakistan
and England playing a game called cricket (see
Appendix A for rules).

During our routine patrols of the perimeter
boundary, we observed some disputes were
occurring between the Pakistan and England
supporters, and we were called upon to break up
fights, quell pitch invasions and answer enquiries
about career opportunities in the police force.

At one point, a Pakistani gentleman
approached me and said, "Excuse me officer, my
throat seems to have been cut", adding that the
injury had been caused by a flying wine bottle
propelled by an England fan. From a preliminary
inspection of his neck, I ascertained that his
jugular vein had indeed been severed, so I
proceeded to stem the flow of blood pulsing from
his neck and called for ambulance back-up.

In the evening, I had a chicken balti pie for
my tea.

Cheater storm stops play

England swamped by deluge of dodgy umpiring decisions

Umpiring is a tough old job, especially when you make lots of dodgy decisions and people start accusing you of being a big old cheater. That's what happened to Shakoor Rana during England's 1987–88 tour of Pakistan.

In the second Test, England captain Mike Gatting and Mr Rana had a stand-up row on the pitch accusing each other of cheating, after Rana reprimanded Gatting for changing his field setting too late (or something).

Rana refused to carry on umpiring (which might not have been such a bad thing …) until Gatting apologised. There was no play on the third day as the argument raged, the only time in cricket history that a cheetah, er, cheater storm has stopped play!

Sledge master Merv

The wit (and moustache) of Merv Hughes

Merv Hughes, an Australian and the owner of a very silly moustache, was a good Test cricketer, but he will be best remembered for his contribution to the art of sledging.

To pick just one tale from a glorious career spent abusing batsmen would be foolish, but as Merv might say, "What the f**k?," so here goes …

When Robin Smith played and missed during a Lord's Test match in 1989, Merv politely informed him, "You can't f**king bat."

Smith then hit Merv for four and replied: "Hey Merv, we make a fine pair. I can't f**king bat and you can't f**king bowl!"

They were like Cannon and Ball, only even funnier.

XXXXing big boozer Boon

Boon sets new Australian record on Sydney–London flight

David Boon MBE scored over 7,000 runs for Australia and grew a very bushy moustache. That would be enough for most mere mortals, but Boonie entered the pantheon of legends when he sank a gut-busting 52 cans of beer on a long-haul flight from Sydney to England in 1989.

Modest Boon denies this ever happened, but official statistics (supplied by the flight attendants) and fellow player Dean Jones indicate that he did indeed shatter the previous Australian record of 46 held by Rodney Marsh.

By the time the plane left Singapore Airport, the pint-sized Tasmanian was ripping the ring-pull off can number 23. Eight hours later, the plane's captain hailed a new record to cheers from his team-mates.

Initially, former record holder Marsh refused to ratify Boon's record, claiming "he'd had a couple while on the ground in Singapore". However, Marsh was carried off the plane, whereas Boon, in Jones's words, "kinda managed to walk".

Boonie was fined AS$5,000 for his fine effort and went on to average over 70 in the Ashes series. Well played, cobber!

Child genius takes a bow

Boy master Sachin takes on the big boys and wins

Waqar Younis, Imran Khan and Wasim Akram of Pakistan formed one of the world's most feared pace attacks of the late '80s and early '90s. Imagine their surprise then, when a 16-year-old kid from Bombay called Sachin Tendulkar hit them all over the park in his debut series.

Like big school bullies, Waqar and co. bowled lots of bouncers at him, once hitting him on the nose, but little Sachin refused to give them his lunch money. Instead, at Karachi in 1989, he became the youngest player ever to score a Test match 50, aged just 16 years and 205 days.

Sachin was captain of India by the age of 23 and became the undisputed Head Prefect of world batsmen. Amusingly, he caned Shane Warne in two Test series (1997–98 and 2000–01) scoring at an average of 111.50 and 108.75, while Warne's wickets cost over 50 apiece.

"I'm having nightmares of Sachin running down the track to belt me," blubbed the Aussie at the time. Ah, diddums.

The worst over ever bowled!

Kiwi oversteps the line and gets carted for 77 runs

Everyone loves Simon Hughes's "Analyst" spot on telly, mainly because it's guaranteed Mark Nicholas-free airtime. But Hawkeye (and maybe even Hughes himself) might have self-combusted tracking an over bowled by Robert Vance for Wellington against Canterbury in Christchurch, New Zealand in 1990.

With a draw looking inevitable, Wellington's stupidly named captain, Ervin McSweeney, ordered Vance to bowl badly to try and encourage Canterbury to go for the win. Vance literally overstepped the mark, deliberately bowling no-balls aimed anywhere but at the stumps and conceding an impressive 77 runs from his 22-ball over.

Analyse that, Simon!

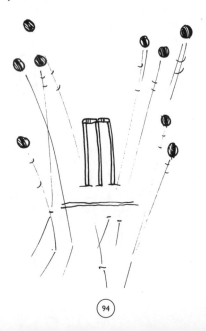

Boffins solve catching conundrum

Two professors ensure no catch will ever be dropped again

IN THE EARLY '90S, TWO EMINENT UNIVERSITY PROFESSORS
I.M.POINTLESS AND L.A.Z.Y. BUGGER WITH NOTHING BETTER
TO DO WITH THEIR LIVES, WATCHED LOADS OF TEST MATCH
VIDEOS AND CAME UP WITH A THEOREM TO JUSTIFY THE
WASTE OF TIME AND MONEY. FOR THE RECORD, THE
FORMULA FOR TAKING A CATCH ON THE RUN IS

$$D^2 \, (TAN \, A)/DT^2 = 0.$$

AND FIELDERS AROUND THE WORLD NEVER DROPPED
A BALL EVER AGAIN, YADDA, YADDA, YADDA...

NOTE: NAMES HAVE
BEEN CHANGED TO SAVE
EMBARRASSMENT.

Gower flies ... in a plane!

Aviator David flies over match Down Under

Now a part-time crisp salesman, David Gower was once
a dashing left-handed batsman with a weakness for
tickling outside off stump. He also had a weakness for
aviation, so when he saw an airfield near the ground
where England were playing in Queensland in January
1991, he couldn't resist.

Team-mate John Morris, also born on April Fool's Day
(no, really), was his chosen co-pilot. With England batting,
they sneaked out of the pavilion, hired two 1938 Tiger
Moth bi-planes and buzzed back and forth over the
cricket pitch. It was all spiffing good fun, but the
spoilsport England management fined the flyaway pair a
grand each.

"It wasn't as if we were far away from the ground,"
protested Gower later. "We were only 150 metres
above it."

The Khan dynasty

Imran wins World Cup and becomes cricketing royalty

In 1992, Pakistan won the World Cup (beating England in the final) led by their brilliant captain Imran Khan. Imran had become the king of Pakistan cricket (although he didn't wear a crown and had no practical governmental powers).

Forty years before, Imran had been born with a silver cricket ball in his mouth, and unless he'd decided to do something completely different, he was always destined to become a cricketer. Eight of his first cousins played first-class cricket (two of them, Majid Khan and Javed Burki, captaining Pakistan) and two of his uncles played for India.

An Oxford Blue, all-rounder Imran was playing for Pakistan while still at university, and went on to do the rare "triple double" of 3,000 runs and 300 wickets in Test cricket.

After winning the World Cup, the King abdicated and moved into the less stressful world of Pakistani politics.

Shane

There's a new sheriff in town ... and he's a blond Australian

No, not the acclaimed Western movie *Shane*. No, this was the slightly more exciting arrival on the Test cricket scene of Australian leg-spinner Shane Warne.

He made an explosive entry into Ashes Tests in summer 1993 by bowling Mike Gatting first ball with a fizzing leg-break. Howdy do that?

Warne took eight wickets in the match and Australia won by 179 runs. His debut performance proved to be a complete fluke though, because by the time Frank Skinner's "hilarious" sitcom *Shane* was aired in 2004, Warne had only managed to add another 500-odd Test wickets to his tally.

Lara scores half a thousand!

It's a Lara, Lara runs, as Cilla might say

In 1959, Karachi star Hanif Mohammed became the first person ever to score 500 runs in a first-class innings on his own ... except he didn't because he got run out on 499! Happily, 35 years later, Brian Lara really did score 500 plus one extra run to make up for poor Hanif's lapse.

In the summer of 1994, left-hander Lara went on a run rampage starting in March when he blasted a record Test score of 375 against England in Antigua (ten years later he would beat this record, and a new world mark of 380 scored by some Australian, scoring 400, again against England, in Antigua).

Then playing for his new county Warwickshire in June '94, Lara bashed an unbeaten 501 in just 427 balls. During his mega innings, Lara was "bowled" from a no-ball on 12, and dropped by the wicket-keeper on 18 – if he had been out either time he really would have scored a lot less runs.

Athers accused

... but the England skipper says claims are a load of balls

Back in 1994, ball-tampering was all the rage in cricket, if you believed the tabloid press. It wasn't just bored fielders jangling with their balls; apparently, everything from bottle tops to pneumatic drills were being used by fielding sides to help the ball to swing.

So when England skipper Mike Atherton was caught on camera rubbing some dust from his pocket on the ball during a Test against South Africa, it caused a right old rumpus.

The incident made TV news headlines, and Athers got fined by England's head honchos.

"I was not altering the condition of the ball; I was trying to maintain its dry and rough condition," explained Athers in his autobiography, warning that he might sue anyone who labels him a cheat ... so we won't, and offer this ludicrous double-entendre cartoon instead ...

"Ooh look, he's tampering with his balls."

Colour-blind third umpire

Should he stay or should he go?

By the 1990s, a "Third Umpire" with a big telly (and a green and red button) had been introduced to help the two umpires on the pitch without one. So when a replay clearly showed that South African batsman Dave Richardson had made his ground taking a quick single during an international against Pakistan in October 1994, third ump Atio Khan knew he was not out. Unfortunately, Mr Khan accidentally pressed the red button for "out". Turns out later that he's colour blind. Oops.

Kenyans shock the West Indies

Richardson and co. toppled by minnows

Cricket's only a game, so it's always nice when a top player shows a sense of perspective. And rarely has a cricketer shown more perspective than West Indies captain Richie Richardson after his team had lost to Kenya in the 1996 World Cup.

Pre-match, the height of the Kenyan players' ambitions was probably to get a few autographs from Brian Lara and co. Instead, the African team, featuring precisely one professional player, managed to bowl out the West Indies for 93 and win by 73 runs!

It was the biggest shock in World Cup cricket history, but while West Indian fans and former players mourned the fall of a great cricketing nation, Richie preferred to look on the bright side.

"It's not the end of the world," he commented brightly, presumably putting the defeat in the context of global famine, pestilence and war.

He was right. The West Indies recovered to reach the semi-finals and Richie promptly resigned before he was sacked.

Sri Lanka pinch the World Cup

New cricketers on the block revolutionise one-day cricket

Sri Lanka were only granted Test status in 1981, but a mere 15 years later the new kids on the cricket block were the best in the world ... well, at one-day cricket anyway.

At the 1996 World Cup, their blazin' squad flip reversed the tradition of steadily building an innings by blazing away from the start to take advantage of new fielding restrictions in the first 15 overs. This so-called "pinch hitting" worked so well in their group match against Kenya that they ran up a world record one-day international score of 398 for 5.

They played favourites Australia in the final in Lahore, and again captain Arjuna Ranatunga audaciously flip reversed by putting the Aussies into bat first (no team batting second had ever won a final before). A brilliant century by Arjuna's main man Aravinda de Silva in the second innings ensured they pinched the trophy.

Sri Lanka had made one-day cricket even better. Sadly, boy bands would always be crap.

Don't have a cow, man!

Security gorillas injure arse end of panto cow

One of the "joys" of going to a Test match these days, is finding yourself sat next to a group of "zany" fans in fancy dress. Nun habits, Elvis wigs, Jonathan Agnew masks… it really is ha-ha-hilarious to see what "madcap" outfit these "crazee" people will wear next.

But getting dressed up can have its hazards, as a two-man pantomime cow discovered when taking a wander on the outfield at Headingley during the fourth Test between England and Australia in 1997. Five witless

gorillas dressed as stewards came from behind (in true panto tradition) to roughly bundle the oblivious bovine impersonators to the ground. The "hind legs" (a man named Branco Risek) emitted a sickening "Moooo" before losing consciousness and getting carted off to hospital.

At the same game, a university lecturer called Brian Cheesman was also ejected from the ground for "drunken and abusive behaviour". Mr Cheesman was dressed as a carrot.

The most dangerous pitch ever!

England batsman black and blue after 62-ball Test match

The first Test match of England's 1998 West Indies tour was played on a re-laid wicket at Sabina Park in Jamaica. The new pitch was a bit bumpy and cracked and looked like it would probably deteriorate as the match went on, so toss-winning England skipper Mike Atherton decided to bat first.

However, West Indies' opening bowlers Curtly Ambrose and Courtney Walsh soon discovered the perfect line and length to bowl (i.e. any line and length) as the ball either jagged up off the Himalayan bumps or caught a glacial crack and shot along the ground.

Physio Wayne Morton was called on to the pitch six times in the first hour as England's batsmen tried not to die. After 66 minutes, with England on 17 for 3 off 62 balls, the umpires and two captains realised that there might not be enough slabs at the local morgue to cope if the game continued. The match was abandoned, the first Test ever to be called off due to a pitch being a death trap. It was a very short day for Test cricket.

"You might as well stand at square leg with me."

In-ger-land's Barmy Army

Aussie media unleash the dogs

England's travelling supporters were first labelled the "Barmy Army" by the Australian media during the 1994–95 Ashes tour. "Barmy" because they were prepared to travel halfway round the world to support a useless team who couldn't win a game; and "Army" because there were lots of them. Geddit?

The Barmy Army have since become renowned for their "songs, chants, irony and wit" (according to the official website) or mindless chanting which spoils other people's enjoyment of the game, depending on your point of view.

On the positive side, it is hard to deny the Aussie-baiting genius of such lyrics as "You all live in a convict colony" to the tune of "Yellow Submarine" or the seminal, "I-Oh! I-Oh! We are the Barmy Boys".

However, some spectators at England's third Test match on the 1998 West Indies tour are still in therapy after being forced to listen to endless Barmy Army renditions of "Who Let The Dogs Out?". Who, indeed?

What's up chuck?

Freaky-armed spinner in "throwing" controversy

Since overarm bowling was first introduced, many a
bowler has been accused of being a bent-arm
"thrower", and during the 1990s, the action of Sri
Lankan spinning genius Muttiah Muralitharan was one
under the microscope.

"Murali" was accused of having a bent action, but it
turned out that he was just born with bent arms. That
didn't deter Aussie umpire Ross Emerson from no-balling
him during a game against England in January 1999. Sri
Lankan captain Arjuna Ranatunga chucked his toys out of
the pram, threatening to take his team off in protest.

Murali went on reach 500 Test match wickets in just
87 Tests. Ho-ho ... you had to chuck-le.

Braver newer world

Think brave and new, and add an "er" on the end

By the late 1990s, it had been scientifically proven that England were crap at cricket. Something needed to be done, and who better than someone who used to work at Tescos to do it?

Former supermarket kingpin Lord MacLaurin produced a report entitled, "Raising the Standard" which provided a blueprint for making lazy-arsed county cricketers actually try to win matches for their money (among other things).

Lord Tesco proposed a "three-conference" scheme, but it was so complicated no one understood how it worked. Instead, in 1999, the one-day Sunday League was divided into two divisions of nine teams with promotion and relegation and a year later the County Championship followed suit.

The Sunday League was radically restructured to become the "National League", and the counties adopted funky new names (ranging from the Essex Eagles to the baffling Somerset Sabres) when they played in it on Sundays. Even better, the players got to wear multi-coloured pyjamas and had their own signature tune played as they came in to bat.

It was brave, it was new, and it was bangin'.

The temptation of Hansie

Icon loses it all for a leather jacket and a lotta rand ...

Outside the S&M community, few people suffered more for their love of leather than the late Hansie Cronje. A born-again Christian, the South African captain was hero-worshipped in his home country and respected around the world. Until April 2000, that is, when he admitted receiving at least $130,000 (and a nice leather jacket) from illegal bookmakers and other dubious characters since 1996. "In a moment of stupidity and weakness I allowed Satan and the world to dictate terms to me," explained Hansie.

He claimed never to have "thrown" or "fixed" a match (hmm), but admitted to an "unfortunate love of money" – so unfortunate that 72 bank accounts in the Cayman Islands held in his name were later discovered. After being banned for life, he was able to put his misfortune to good use, taking a job as a financial manager.

Tragically, Cronje was killed in a plane crash two years later and his sins were forgiven by the majority of South Africans. "He will be remembered as a great captain and a great person," said former team-mate Andrew Hudson.

Er, amen to that.

Waugh, what is he good for?

… er, quite a lot, really …

Kangaroos were skipping for joy on 3 January 2003, as Aussie skipper Steve Waugh became only the third man to reach 10,000 runs in Test cricket. He reached the landmark on the second day of the fifth Test against England, and went on to hit a four off the last ball of the day to complete his 29th Test century, equalling Sir Don Bradman's record.

Apart from batting, what was Waugh good for? Well, he was a born leader (he was born four minutes before his cricketing twin brother Mark) and in his five years as Test captain, Australia once won 16 Tests in a row and became the best team in the world. He also found time to set up a charity for the daughters of lepers in Calcutta. Good for quite a lot, then.

Steve eventually hung up his baggy green cap in 2004 as the most capped player (168 Tests) in history. That's a whole lotta caps.

Fat boy slim

Blubbery Shane loses inches (and World Cup place) on dodgy diet plan

Shane Warne has always had problems with regulations.

During a tour of Sri Lanka in 1994, he accepted money from an illegal bookmaker, allegedly for giving pitch information. Shane copped a fine but proclaimed his innocence, saying the money he received was just "a token of appreciation".

Then, in 1996, Shane was photographed puffing on a ciggie after the former 40-a-day man had signed a AS$200,000 deal pledging not to smoke for four months. Shane claimed it was "a mere blip".

The disciplines of a calorie-controlled diet have habitually posed difficulties too. But when he turned up (rather than rolled up) for the 2003 World Cup having slimmed down from a 36-inch to a 32-inch waist in a year, it seemed that he'd finally found a way to lose the surplus chins. A pesky doping test revealed that way was taking a banned diuretic. Slim Shane was forced to withdraw from the tournament and banned for a year.

Oops, he'd blipped again!

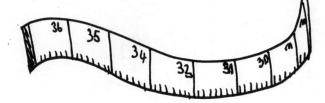

Master of the mic no.2: Richie

Yes, got 'im!

The late, great commentator Richie Benaud OBE will undoubtedly go down in cricketing history as one of the few Australians that English people have actually liked.

The moment the former leg-spinning all-rounder's lovely froggish face appeared on screen and he uttered the words "Morning everyone" in his distinctive tones (and Mark Nicholas got his big fat ego out of the way) cricket fans knew it really was game on.

Richie didn't earn his "The Voice of Cricket" nickname for nothing, and you could always rely on him to find just the right words (and a smart cream jacket) for any occasion.

Renowned for his sharp, incisive commentary, he had the rare gift of letting the pictures speak for themselves except when they were misleading ("That slow motion doesn't show how fast the ball was travelling") or breaking down the complexities of the scorecard for the viewers ("There were no scores below single figures").

Richie, God rest your soul, we salute you.

Twenty20 vision

New competition proves to be a brilliant spectacle

With the success of National League pyjama cricket matches between teams with silly names, even the traditionalists were saying bugger to tradition. Now they had 20–20 vision of the game's future, a glorious vision of a modern game in which batsmen slogged the ball indiscriminately, music blared out, cheerleaders danced and hordes of modern fans with attention deficiency disorders cheered and bought more beer.

So it was in 2003 that the first 20-over-a-side Twenty20 Cup was introduced. There were penalties for

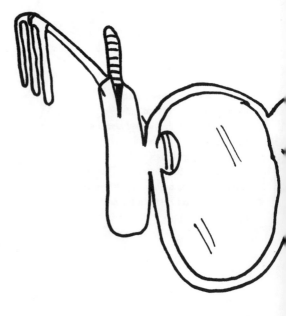

bowling or batting too slowly, no-balls were punished with a free hit next ball and players would generally rush around being entertaining for the three hours or less it took to play a game.

The Twenty20 Cup paved the way for loads more twenty-over competitions like the glitzy Indian Premier League, Australia's Big Bash League and England's T20 Blast (which is the Twenty20 Cup, only with a better name). All in all, Twenty20 has proved to be a thrilling spectacle.

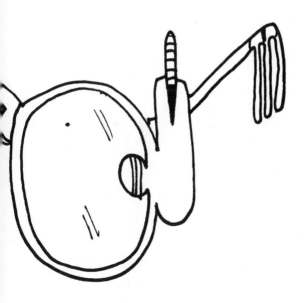

Tuffers is King of the Jungle

Beetle-eating "Cat" creates cricket history by winning reality TV show

1966 was a great year for English cricket: Philip Clive Roderick Tufnell was born. Nicknamed "Cat" (for his ability to sleep anywhere, not his less-than-feline reflexes), Tuffers's decade-long Test career began in 1990 and he went on to take 121 wickets at an average of 37. Okay, maybe the stats aren't Warne-esque, but being the bad boy of English cricket is no walk in the park. Hell, you try to bowl spin when you've got an ex-girlfriend's father running after you with a brick.

Life was never dull with Tuffers around and he became a cult hero among England fans for his extra-curricular antics, comedy batting and occasional match-winning bowling displays. Then after retiring from cricket, Cat made cricket history in the Australian jungle, becoming the first cricketer to win a reality TV show. His roguish charm and ability to eat live wichetty grubs earned him the *I'm A Celebrity … Get Me Out Of Here* "King of the Jungle" crown.

Back to the future!

Freddie leads England's charge back to the pinnacle of world cricket (for a while) …

After years of being rubbish, the new millennium heralded the start of an exciting new era for the English cricket team. Under new captain Michael Vaughan, England started to enjoy the novel experience of winning. They liked the feeling so much that in summer 2004 they won seven Tests in a row and suddenly, England were better than Australia again (possibly).

Then, the following summer England proved they were actually better than the Aussies, thrashing them 2–1 in arguably the most exciting Test series ever to reclaim the Ashes for the first time since 1987. A year and a half later, England emphasized their new-found superiority by going Down Under and … oh, getting mullered 5–0.

Never mind about that, though. Straussy, Harmy, KP, Gilo … every man played a part in the magical revival, but no-one captured the fans' imagination more than mighty all-rounder Andrew "Freddie" Flintoff. Nicknamed after a prehistoric cartoon caveman, when big Freddie wasn't busy skittling out the Aussies, he was clubbing the ball out of the ground. Yabba-dabba dooo …

False messiah lands at cricket Mecca

Cricket sells wits soul to fraudst… er, billionaire Allen Stanford

June 2008: a Texan billionaire called Allen Stanford lands his helicopter on Lord's hallowed turf, poses with Sirs Ian Botham and Viv Richards next to a box supposedly containing $20 million cash – the prize he's offering for a single Twenty20 game between England and Stanford Superstars (or the West Indies as they had previously been known) – and he declares that Test cricket is "boring" … what could possibly go wrong?

The powers-that-be at the English Cricket Board (ECB) and the West Indies board weren't thinking about the negatives – perhaps because of the additional $3.5 million each Stanford was paying into their coffers. Neither were the players, who were busy clawing each other for the chance to play and win $1 million per man.

The first of the five planned annual festivals of avarice

– sorry, Stanford Super Series $20 million matches – was played in Antigua on 1 November and while Stanford flirted with England players' WAGs, Stanford Superstars won the booty.

A few months later, it came to light that Stanford's multi-billion-dollar business was actually a massive Ponzi scheme. All contracts for future matches were cancelled, and the fraudster who once owned a 112-feet-long motor yacht got sentenced to a 110-year stretch in prison.

Eagle-eyed umpires get help from Hawk-Eye and co.

The Umpire Decision Review System is introduced

Once upon a time, a batsman who took a decent stride down the pitch with his front foot and got rapped on the pad could be pretty sure he wouldn't be given out lbw even if the ball was dead straight. Spinners rarely even bothered to appeal for fear of a disdainful response from the umpire. However, in 2002, when Hawk-Eye ball-tracking technology was introduced for the benefit of TV viewers, who could then belatedly bitch and moan about incorrect umpiring decisions, it was clear that some of those "Not Out" decisions may well have been "Outs". Within just six years, the ICC Cricket Committee realised it might be an awfully good idea to use Hawk-Eye to actually review controversial umpiring decisions and correct errors. Thus, the Umpire Decision Review System (UDRS, but usually called DRS) was officially launched in 2009. Now the batter, fielding team captain or on-field umpire has to make a "T" shape with their arms to ask for the Third Umpire to check Hawk-Eye, Hot Spot (infra-red imaging system showing if the ball contacts bat or pad) and or/the Snickometer (to detect small sounds made by ball on bat or pad). Perhaps the ICC felt it would be too Village People to make the full "U", "D", "R" and "S" shapes every time a decision was referred.

Barmy Broom cycles to Oz

Daft-as-a-brush England fan pedals from Lord's to the Gabba

There are some barmy ways to make the long trip from England to Australia, but few barmier options than cycling there. And yet that is how Oli Broom – ironically, not a member of the Barmy Army – made his way to the 2010/11 Ashes series.

Broom began his epic bike ride from Lord's cricket ground, carrying only essential possessions like his cricket bat. He nearly gave up with a sore knee before he reached the English coast, but bravely pedalled on for 412 days, covering 14,000 miles across 23 countries on four continents, to arrive just in time for the first Test at the Gabba in Brisbane.

England skipper Andrew Strauss was there waiting to give Broom a signed England shirt, and he'd raised 75 grand for charity along the way, clear evidence that the whole thing hadn't been a staggering waste of time.

Having survived being knocked off his bike by a truck in Bulgaria and a bout of dengue fever in Thailand, poor Broom didn't emerge completely unscathed from his cyclo-cricket pilgrimage. While playing for the MCC in a game at the MCG the day after England retained the Ashes there, he dived forward to catch a ball off John Emburey's bowling and snapped a finger.

Cricketer comes out

Wicket-keeper announces he is gay … and meets Coldplay

It's hard to believe that until 2011, official statistics showed that there had never been a homosexual professional cricketer … well, not so much hard to believe as patently absurd and a poor reflection on the sport that many cricketers have felt unable to be honest about their sexuality.

When Surrey and England wicket-keeper Steven Davies publicly announced he is gay in February of that year, he described taking the step as being as nerve-wracking as facing fearsome Aussie fast bowler Brett Lee in the middle.

Among hundreds of letters from people thanking him for breaking new ground was one from Sir Elton John (who also sent a couple of bottles of champagne for good measure). The pair became friends and Steven joined the pop legend on tour. "One time I walked into his suite and Elton was in there having coffee with Coldplay," he recalls. Thankfully, Coldplay didn't start playing their songs.

Master of the mic No.3: Aggers

Agnew delivers impromptu sex education lesson

Twenty years after he and Brian "Johnners" Johnston famously corpsed on live radio (see page 72), Aggers again accidentally turned the air blue on *Test Match Special*. Aggers was commentating with Michael Vaughan on the final day of the second Test between England and Sri Lanka at Lord's in 2011 when a drinks break was called because Kevin Pietersen needed a new rubber on his bat handle.

"As all amateurs will know, it is not easy to do that," notes Aggers innocently. "You've got to roll it down the stick and make sure it is all in place, and no floppy stuff on the end of the handle – you can't have that … Michael Vaughan is beside me – it's not easy putting on a rubber is it?"

"No, it's not – I was never good at that," replies Vaughan drily before he and everyone else in the *TMS* box burst out laughing.

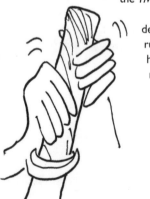

Finally, realising why his detailed appraisal of KP's rubber-rolling technique has caused such merriment, Aggers responds: "You know what I meant …"

Yes, we do, Aggers. Put simply: be safe, kids.

Sachin hits ton of tons

Little Master sets 100 x 100 milestone that may never be beaten

Remember that child genius Sachin Tendulkar we were banging on about on page 93? Well, class swot Sachin grew up to a height of 5ft 5in, and became not only the undisputed god of Indian cricket, but one of the record-breaking-est batsmen in world cricket history.

He finally retired from all forms in 2013 aged 40, having scored 34,357 runs in 664 international cricket matches, thus sparing bowlers further embarrassment.

To mention just a couple of his international career records, the "Little Master" was the first man to score more than 30,000 runs and the first batsman to score a double century in a One Day International. Greatest of all, on 16 March 2012 at 5.05pm local time against Bangladesh at the Shere Bangla stadium in Mirpa, Sachin notched his hundredth international ton. If only Roy Castle had been alive to see it, he would have tap-danced around Norris McWhirter and played the *Record Breakers* theme tune a hundred times on his trumpet in tribute, oh yes.

The reintegration (and disintegration) of KP

Pietersen spins in and out of the ECB's revolving door

To some, Kevin Pietersen is the greatest English batsman of his generation. To others, he is a "complete c***", as his former captain Andrew Strauss once was heard calling him when he thought his microphone was turned off. The fact that he reached 4,000, 5,000 and 7,000 Test runs faster (in terms of days) than any player in history backs up the former school of thought, while his association with Piers Morgan lends weight to the latter.

In 2009, a rift with England coach Peter Moores led to KP being told to resign as captain by the ECB. Worse was to follow in the summer of 2012 when he was dropped after allegations that he sent text messages with defamatory comments about his own team-mates and new coach Andy Flower to members of the opposing South African team.

A few months later, the ECB announced Kev would be reintegrated into the side, but after the disastrous 2013/14 Ashes tour where he batted almost as badly as everyone else, he was disintegrated again. KP then released an autobiography that made playing for England sound about as much fun as being a prefect's fag at a boarding school. The chances of another reintegration looked slim, but given KP's bouncebackability, he might be back in the team by the time you read this.

Fat's amazing!

Aussie stars eat more fat to get thin

Present-day professional cricket requires "3D players", finely tuned athletes who can bat, bowl and field. It's a big change from the good old days when some players were more three-dimensional than others by virtue of the amount of pints they consumed after close of play.

Aside from hours of training, it's vital to stick to a strict diet to stay in shape, which players are often told means laying off the fatty foods and "carb-loading" for energy. Not for stars of the Australian cricket team though since 2012/13 when their team doctor Peter Brukner lost 12kg in 12 weeks on a low-carb, low-sugar but high-fat diet. Shane "Watto" Watson, Mitchell Johnson and David Warner among others – who had all been struggling to stay slim despite working their lardy backsides off and eating "properly" – asked the Doc for the secret of his newly svelte figure. Much to their delight, they discovered it was pigging out on steaks, eggs, full-fat cream, milk and cheese.

"It's hard to get your head around the fact that the more fat you eat, the more fat you lose," says Doc B.

Not for Watto, who tucked into the new diet for 18 months, and found he got slimmer, more energetic and less grumpy. It didn't seem to do Johnson and Warner any harm either as they, respectively, took the most wickets and scored the most runs for Oz in their 5–0 2013/14 Ashes series drubbing of England. Fat's the way to do it!

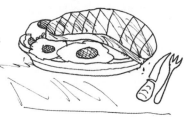

Cricket at the highest level

Record-breaking match played on the "roof of Africa"

As anyone who's ever done online dating knows, if you don't say on your profile that you've climbed Mount Kilimanjaro or dream of doing so, you ain't getting a date. And judging by the amount of people on match.com claiming to have ascended Tanzania's mega-mountain, you'd think it was quite easy. Apparently not though – it actually requires an exhausting week-long trek to reach the "roof of Africa", where the air is so thin you can hardly breathe and the temperature is about 20 below. Not ideal conditions for cricket there then, but there cricket's highest-ever match was played (well, near the summit on a flattish bit at 5,752 metres above sea level) in September 2014, beating the previous record set by a game on a little hillock called Mount Everest five years before.

"Next time you hit a six you can f***ing get it!"

A team led by England women's international Heather Knight wheezed to victory over former "King of Spain" Ashley Giles's side on Mount Kili, and the single members of both teams returned home with their online dating credentials hugely enhanced.

Absolutely smashing it!

Big-hitters Gayle, De Villiers and Guptill have spectators diving for cover at World Cup 2015

Nowadays, One Day Internationals seem pedestrian in comparison to Twenty20 matches. But at the 2015 World Cup, Chris Gayle, A.B. de Villiers and Martin Guptill played innings violent enough to keep even the most hardcore T20 fan awake.

In the Pool B match against Zimbabwe in Canberra, West Indies opener Gayle biffed 215 runs off 147 balls – the first double century ever in a World Cup match and the fastest-ever ODI double-ton. No T20-style ramp or reverse-lap shots for big Chris who instead focused on brutal thwacks for his 16 sixes.

A few days later in Sydney, A.B. de Villiers walloped the Windies attack for the fastest-ever 150 in an ODI off just 64 balls. A.B. finished with 162 not out off 66 balls, including 17 fours and eight sixes as South Africa romped to victory by 257 runs (another World Cup record).

Then, in the quarter-final in Wellington, Guptill smashed the Windies attack for 237 not out, clouting 11 sixes and breaking Gayle's record for highest World Cup innings. New Zealand won easily, but Gayle went down fighting, clubbing eight sixes in an innings of 61 to take his total to a tournament-record 26 sixes.

Oh yes, cricket has come a very long way since the Middle Ages when English rural yokels hit cats with planks ...

Other titles in this series include:

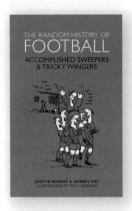

ISBN 978-1-85375-936-9

ISBN 978-1-85375-938-3

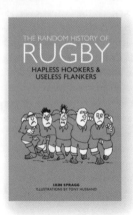

ISBN 978-1-85375-939-0